Bûcheron

Crogham

re de Touraine

Taupinière

Chèvre de Bellay

Goat Cheese

[Delectable Recipes for All Occasions]

BY ETHEL BRENNAN AND GEORGEANNE BRENNAN

ILLUSTRATIONS BY PHILIPPE WEISBECKER

CHRONICLE BOOKS

SAN FRANCISCO

Library of Congress Cataloging-in-Publication Data:
Brennan, Ethel.
        Goat cheese: delectable recipes for all occasions/by Ethel Brennan and
Georgeanne Brennan; illustrations by Philippe Weisbecker.
            p. cm.
        Includes index.
        ISBN 0-8118-1239-1 (hc)
        1. Cookery (Goat cheese) 2. Goat cheese. I. Brennan, Georgeanne, 1943–. II. Title.
        TX759.5.C48B74 1997
        641.6'7353—dc20
                                96-28039
                                CIP

Printed in Hong Kong

Illustrations: Philippe Weisbecker
Design: Gretchen Scoble

Distributed in Canada by Raincoast Books
8680 Cambie Street
Vancouver, B.C. V6P 6M9

10 9 8 7 6 5 4 3 2 1

Chronicle Books
85 Second Street
San Francisco, CA 94105

Web Site: www.chronbooks.com

ACKNOWLEDGEMENTS

Special thanks to Stephen Schack and Jennifer Lynn Bice
of Redwood Hill Farm for their constant support and their great cheeses,
Spencer Pexton of North Coast Dairy Goats for his fine cheeses, Frances Andrews
and Nigel Walker of Eatwell Farm for their excellent produce, Barbara Backus of
Goats' Leap Farm for her enthusiasm and support, Pierre Kolisch
of Juniper Grove Dairy, Jana McAninch for her love of cheesecake,
Sharon Spain for her love of goat cheese, Jordan Grothe,
M. and Mme Caplan, M. and Mme Chabot,
Luc and Nelly, Bill LeBlond, Leslie Jonath, Sharon Silva,
and special thanks to Donald Brennan.

INTRODUCTION

The goat has long held a place in the annals of history and the legends of mythology. It was worshipped by the ancient Egyptians, yet feared by the Christians of the Middle Ages who associated it with the evil of Satan. Greek mythology tells the story of the *cornucopia,* the horn from the goat nymph Amalthea that was filled with an inexhaustible supply of fruits, vegetables, and grains. Zeus made a gift of the magical horn to the daughters of King Melisseus, who had cared for him during his infancy. Even goats' milk cheese has created its own body of lore. It is said, for example, that a goat cheese made in the old Roman province of Provence was so rich and strong, and so loved by the unsuspecting Emperor Antononius Pius, that he overindulged and subsequently died from his gluttony.

Goats are independent and curious creatures, qualities that have translated into a reputation for being mischievous and clever. The word *capricious,* from the Latin *capre,* or "goat," means unpredictable and impulsive. Anyone who has ever owned goats will attest to their superior intelligence and remarkably human personality traits. A strong character, combined with rugged survivalist instincts, have made them highly adaptable, and as a result goats exist in all corners of the world, far from their places of origin in the Middle East and Asia. The ability of goats to endure and flourish in both desert and mountain climates has made them indispensable as milk-producing herd animals in places where cattle raising is difficult, if not impossible.

Dairy Goats and Cheese Production Although France is the country most commonly associated with goat cheeses, we can also find imported goats' milk cheeses from a handful of other European nations. Greece and Turkey (as well as Israel) produce salty goats' milk feta, which tends to be milder than its sheeps' milk counterpart. Northern European countries produce semisoft and hard cheeses such as a Dutch goats' milk Gouda and a slightly sweet, caramelized Norwegian *gjetost,* while in the south, Italians make *caprino,* a Romano-style cheese. In other areas of the world, including countries in Africa, Asia,

and South America, goats are indispensable sources of meat and cheese, but the cheeses are not exported. Indeed, many goat cheeses from all parts of the world, including France and the United States, are produced on such a small scale that they never reach farther than local marketplaces.

France produces more goats' milk and goats' milk cheese for the commercial market, including export, than any other country in the world. *Fromage de chèvre* translates as "goat cheese," although in the United States, the *fromage de* is often dropped and a soft-fresh goat cheese is commonly referred to simply as *chèvre,* literally "goat."

A French goat farm is an *élevage des chèvres,* and it can be a small family-run dairy of sixty to seventy head, or an operation that houses thousands of goats and yields hundreds of thousands of liters of milk each year. Throughout France, from the rocky, rosemary-covered hills of Provence, to the towering Alps, to the valleys of the Loire, one can find goat farms of all sizes that produce a wide range of rich and flavorful cheeses, some for export, but most for domestic consumption.

Many French goats are still raised by the traditional method of herding, in which the animals spend the day roaming the open countryside with a goatherd. These goats have the luxury of feeding upon the wild vegetation of their region. In Provence, they feast on the juniper, sage, thyme, and grasses that grow freely throughout the abandoned olive and chestnut orchards and across the slopes of the lower Alps. In the central grasslands, they are fenced into more conventional dairy environments, where they graze the meadows in the absence of the watchful eye of a goatherd. These goats enjoy a diet of sweet grasses supplemented with hearty grains. As a result, they often have a much higher milk yield than the rugged foraging goats of southern France. It is no surprise, then, that this region produces the majority of the country's goats' milk and cheese.

During the spring, some southern herdsmen walk with their goats and sheep from the lowlands of Provence to the high Alps, repeating a tradition called transhumance that has been in practice since the fifteenth century. It developed from the need to augment the diet of herd animals dependent upon the changing seasons. The dry, hot summers of Provence deplete the region of the desirable wild grasses, so the shepherds move their animals north to escape the heat and to seek better grazing lands. With the first signs of fall, the herdsmen lead the goats and sheep back to Provence. Now, however, with modernization, shepherds and their animals are more often traveling to and from the mountains by truck rather than by foot.

Life as a Provençal Goatherd In the early 1970s, our family wanted to live and work in Provence, and a herd of goats became our means for making a living. We first gathered information from local producers, and soon after the craft of making traditional goats' milk cheese was our livelihood. Our goats, among them the very gentle and affectionate Café au Lait and the more lively, independent Bon Marché, were milked twice a day, once early in the morning and again in the evening when they returned from a day of foraging in the forest and meadows.

The milk was strained and the coagulant rennet was added to it to promote the separation into solid curds and watery whey. The curds were then ladled into ceramic or plastic molds and allowed to drain. Within a day, the fresh cheeses were rotated. The next day, the cheeses were removed from the molds, lightly salted, and transferred to a fine-mesh wire rack to continue draining. A day later, the fresh, sweet cheeses were ready to be wrapped in waxed paper and taken to the local open market where we sold them.

After a short time, our cheeses had gained a good reputation in the region, and people began arriving at our house daily to buy up to a dozen of them at a time. Eventually, a wholesaler from the city of Toulon found our little farm, and soon we were selling him hundreds of cheeses each week. A portion of our fresh cheeses was set aside to age for a week or two, forming a velvety white mold on the outside and a dense, creamy interior. Others were left to age even longer, becoming hard and dry before they were sold.

When we returned to the United States in 1973, we craved the flavorful cheeses we had grown accustomed to eating daily. Unfortunately, goat cheese as we knew it was virtually nonexistent in this country at that time. The recent development of small goat dairies and of the commercial production of goat cheese in the United States can be credited to Napa

Valley–based cheese maker Laura Chenel. In the late 1970s, Chenel had the vision to import the traditions of French goat-cheese making to California, after studying its production in France. Now there exist about two hundred small goat dairies across the country.

La Transhumance

Goat Cheese Production in the United States In America, specialty goat cheeses are primarily manufactured on what are known as farmsteads. The term *farmstead* is used to define small goat, sheep, or cow dairies that make cheeses primarily from the milk of their own animals. Sometimes these cheese makers supplement their production with milk purchased from larger operations that raise animals exclusively for milk. The wide range of cheeses turned out by these small-scale producers are commonly referred to as farmstead cheeses.

Farmsteads from West Virginia and Wisconsin to upstate New York, Indiana, California, and Oregon frequently make goat cheeses that emulate classic French or other European products. In markets, ash-dusted pyramids made in New York or California sit alongside those imported from France, for example, and imported *crottin de Chavignol* and *bûcheron* are shelved next to their domestic versions. Camembert, Cheddar, and Jack cheeses, traditionally made from cows' milk, are instead being made from goats' milk. But the new breed of American goat-cheese makers are not simply copiers. They are also innovators: Jack laced with pine nuts, disks dusted with dried herbs or black peppercorns, soft logs rolled in fresh flowers, and soft-fresh cheese swirled with smoked salmon or dried tomatoes are just a handful of their many creations.

Some of these specialty goat cheeses are sold only at local farmers' markets, or direct from the farm, as are many or the specialty cheeses in France. A number of domestically made goat cheeses, however, are finding their way into cheese shops, specialty-food markets, and supermarkets across the nation, and many producers sell their goat cheeses by mail order (see page 68).

L'affinage

Le moulage

L'emballage

Types of Goat Cheese Goat cheeses are grouped into four basic categories: soft-fresh, semisoft, surface-ripened, and hard-aged. These categories give American cheese buyers a descriptive vocabulary that helps them to distinguish the predominant characteristics present in the thirty-five to forty different types of goat cheeses, both American made and imported, that regularly appear in today's market.

[SOFT-FRESH CHEESES] are anywhere from a few days old up to two weeks old. Their texture is spreadable and somewhat creamy, although not as smooth as cream cheese, and their color is usually a pure white. The intensity of flavor of any soft goat cheese depends upon the age of the cheese. Cheeses in this category tend to be sweeter and milder than the longer-aged surface-ripened types. As the soft-fresh cheeses begin to ripen, their flavors become a little stronger, turning slightly tangy and distinctively aromatic. The texture of these cheeses at the peak of consumption remains spreadable. If left to age, they become somewhat dry and crumbly.

The surface of soft-fresh cheeses can be plain or covered with a fine, edible bluish gray ash or fresh or dried herbs. They are sold in many forms as well: logs, small tubs, cylinders, truncated pyramids, disks, or small buttons. If vacuum-packed, their shelf life, whether domestic or imported, can be up to several months. Cheeses to look for in this category include *taupinière, fromage blanc* or *fromage frais,* ash-covered pyramids (often called *Valençay* if imported from France), and various offerings that are mixed or coated with such herbs as chives, dill, or herbes de Provence.

[SEMISOFT CHEESES] are fresh but not spreadable. Feta falls into this category, as do *queso fresco* (similar to an imported Mexican cows' milk cheese), which has a tangy flavor and a firm texture; a goats' milk Cheddar; and the French *chevrotin,* which is reminiscent of Jack cheese. These cheeses tend to be dense and cuttable and have a mild but not bland flavor; some have rinds.

[SURFACE-RIPENED CHEESES,] also called soft-ripened cheeses, are typically defined by a velvety exterior of mold, or bloom, that is usually white and wrinkled. This mold, however, can also be yellowish brown or grayish blue, or a combination of colors. The mold-ripened cheeses, which tend to be stronger in flavor than the two already-discussed categories, develop a creamy lining between the soft mold and the dense, smooth interior. As is the case with their soft-fresh kin, these cheeses should be served at room temperature so that their textures soften and their full flavor is allowed to come forth. They are also sometimes preserved by storing in olive oil, or wrapped in grape or chestnut leaves to age. In general, surface-ripened goat cheeses are difficult to find in the United States. As they become more popular, however, they will also become more available.

Some domestic producers turn out creamy, somewhat spreadable mold-ripened goats' milk blue cheeses, which tend to be a little milder than other blues. They are made by adding the mold *penicillium Roquefort* to firm curds. Once the curds form cheese, the cheese is pierced with skewers (sometimes coated with mold) to encourage mold growth throughout. The resulting products have mold-ripened rinds and marbled interiors. These blues tend to be marketed and labeled under the names of their specific producers' farms or dairies.

The fourth category is [HARD-AGED CHEESES.] Here, we find both firm, cuttable cheeses similar to Gruyère, and *chèvres secs,* hard, dry cheeses that recall the texture of Romano or Parmesan. The *chèvres secs* are extremely dry and dense, and their flavor is strong and pungent, commonly described in French as *piquant.* To make these hard cheeses, the milk is heated and then treated to remove as much moisture—whey and butter fat—as possible. Next, the cheeses are pressed, coated with wax or salted, and then aged from one month to a year. Although hard-aged goat cheeses are made in a different fashion than surface-ripened and soft-fresh ones, a soft cheese, if left to age properly, can also become hard and dry. The *crottin* is an example of a hard-aged cheese that began as a soft-fresh, was mold-ripened, and finally developed into a dry grating cheese.

A Goat Cheese Sampler The names of goat cheeses can be confusing. Hundreds of different imported and domestic goat cheese varieties exist; some of them are unique to a single producer and are called whatever that producer decides. Thus, there is only one producer for a particular cheese by that name. Other goat cheeses, again both imported and domestic, are made in a recognized style and are called by that name: *crottin,* Camembert, and Banon, for example. In a third consideration, some French goat cheeses are entitled to the AOC *(Appellation d'Origine Contrôlée)* labeling, which means that they are made in a certain place, according to very specific rules and methods that guarantee the purchaser a particular quality. Those names may not otherwise be legally used. For example, *crottin de Chavignol* is an AOC cheese, and although other cheeses may be called *crottin,* only those from Chavignol meet the government standards that allow them to bear the name of the region as well. A further twist is that a number of cheeses traditionally made from cows' milk are also made from goats' milk, both in the United States and in Europe. Goats' milk Camembert, Cheddar, and Banon are examples.

The list that follows is a guide to some of the most common goat cheeses one is likely to find, both domestic and imported.

[B A N O N] This famous French Provençal product is traditionally wrapped in golden brown chestnut leaves that have been dipped in vinegar or eau-de-vie. The leaves are tied in place with raffia, and the cheese is left to age in a cool, dry cellar for three to five weeks. The result is a creamy aged cheese with a rich, earthy flavor, a semihard rind, and a soft, gooey interior. Imported and domestic.

[B û C H E R O N] Sold by the slice cut from a large log about four inches in diameter, this slightly aged surface-ripened French cheese has a gooey, yellowish rind and faint lemony flavor. This is a popular French import, and is also available in domestic versions.

[CAMEMBERT] This surface-ripened French cheese with a white rind is produced in small disks four to five inches in diameter and is sold in individual, round wooden or cardboard boxes. The texture is creamy and smooth, and the flavor is usually strong with a faint aftertaste of hay. Primarily domestic, with some imports.

[CHEDDAR] This familiar semisoft white domestic cheese has a mild flavor and smooth texture.

[CHÈVRE DE BELLAY] Like *bûcheron,* this soft-fresh French cheese is sold in slices cut from a log about four inches in diameter. The texture is slightly grainy and spreadable, and the mild taste is that of a standard soft-fresh goat cheese. A popular import readily available in specialty cheese stores; domestic products are rare.

[COURTURIER] Mild in flavor, this soft-fresh French cheese is sold in logs, either plain or covered in ash or herbs. Sold vacuum-packed, it is available nationwide. Imported.

[CROGHAN] Produced in disks five to six inches in diameter, this is a semisoft Irish cheese with a hard rind, a strong, smoky flavor, and a slightly sour aftertaste. The texture is firm, with a faint lacing of holes throughout. Imported.

[CROTTIN DE CHAVIGNOL] This imported, surface-ripened French AOC cheese is available in two forms: very hard and dry or with a gooey, soft mold-dusted exterior and a firmer center. As the *crottin* ages, it becomes a small, golden one-and-a-half-inch disk with a dry, crumbly texture and sharp flavor. It is considered one of the strongest-flavored goat cheeses (an acquired taste for some) and can be grated when hard and dry. Domestic *crottin* is available.

[FETA] A favorite from Greece, this semisoft cheese tends to be salty and mild, while the texture is somewhat dry and crumbly. Domestic and imported.

[FROMAGE BLANC] Translated literally as "white cheese," this is a soft-fresh cheese typically sold very fresh, not more than a few days old. The flavor is mild and somewhat sweet. Domestic versions are difficult to find, and imports are even rarer.

[GJETOST] The word *ekte* (genuine) on the package ensures that this Norwegian cheese is made from goats' milk only, rather than a blend of goats' and cows' milk. This is a semi-hard cheese made by boiling down the milk until the solids begin to caramelize. The result is a smooth, dark reddish-brown cheese with a sweet and smoky flavor that carries a definite hint of caramel. It is produced in blocks. Imported.

[GOUDA] A popular Dutch cows' milk cheese, Gouda is also occasionally made from goats' milk, resulting in a smooth, firm texture and, unlike its yellowish orange cows' milk cousin, a creamy color. The flavor has a distinctive goats' milk taste, yet is milder than traditional Gouda. Imported.

Soft-ripened cheeses stored in olive oil

[JACK] A common semisoft white cheese that has a mild, creamy flavor when made with goats' milk. Domestic.

[MONTRACHET] A soft-fresh cheese with a creamy texture and a mild flavor, this common French product is sold in logs and is readily available here. Imported.

Le Pélardon

Le Marchand de Fromages

[M O N T S A I N T - F R A N C I S] Sold in six- to eight-inch rounds, this soft-ripened French cheese has a hard rind, usually of orangish yellow. The cheese just beneath the surface is soft, but becomes firmer toward the center, making it both sliceable and spreadable. The flavor is mild and buttery. Imported.

[S A I N T E - M A U R E D E T O U R A I N E] Available in four-to six-inch logs, this surface-ripened French AOC cheese can have a very fine, blue- or pink-tinged rind, or a thicker covering of mold, more like that of a Camembert. Depending upon its age, Sainte-Maure is either smooth and slightly dry or very sharp with a peppery bite and a slightly sour aftertaste. Imported.

[T A U P I N I È R E] This soft-fresh French cheese has a truncated pyramid shape and is often coated in bluish-gray ash. Imported and domestic.

[V A L E N Ç A Y] Readily identifiable by its truncated pyramid shape, this surfaced-ripened French cheese is about three inches high. Depending upon the method of production, Valençay is either plain or covered in wood ash or charcoal, which helps hold in moisture. These cheeses tend to be dark gray or bluish, and sometimes have a surface bloom. Imported and domestic.

Cooking, Serving, and Storing Goat Cheeses

Goat cheeses are extremely versatile in cooking, especially the soft-fresh types. The latter cheeses mix well with other ingredients, particularly in dishes that are baked or broiled. The freshest goat cheeses are so mild, with just a hint of the cheeses' unique taste, that they can be combined with other ingredients in the making of desserts, or they can be served plain with homemade preserves or poached fruit to cap off a meal. Spoonfuls of a sweet soft-fresh cheese *(fromage blanc)* can also be swirled into hot chocolate sauces or spread onto a toasted bagel with a favorite jam or honey.

In contrast, surface-ripened goat cheeses are so rich and so distinctively flavored and textured that they tend to be less flexible in the kitchen. They usually have blooms and hard exterior rinds, however, so they take to baking, holding their shapes while their interiors soften. Semisoft cheeses such as feta, Jack, and Cheddar are excellent for making sauces, as they melt smoothly. Longer-aged cheeses are more piquant and can be used in dishes as flavor enhancers. A few teaspoons of crumbled *crottin* in a warm tomato-and-pasta salad or a creamy salad dressing can impart a pleasant edge to the dish.

Because goats' milk is lower in fat than cows' milk, it produces cheeses that are lighter in texture. As a result, when cooking with goat cheese, whether making sauces or gratins or baking sweets, the finished dishes will not have the heavy oiliness associated with many cows' milk cheese.

When availability allows, a sampling of different goat cheeses—from soft-fresh through hard-aged—makes an elegant dessert platter (see page 64). The cheeses should be served at room temperature to showcase their flavors and textures.

In general, unless you are trying to encourage the aging of soft-fresh cheeses, store goat cheeses by wrapping and then refrigerating them. Use aluminum foil or plastic wrap to retain as much moisture as possible. The cheese should last several weeks, if not months, depending upon the variety. A goat cheese that is no longer good will have a strong, unpleasant smell and taste very sour, even bitter. Although one might argue there exists a fine line between a perfectly aged goat cheese and one that is past its prime, a cheese that is no longer edible will be obviously so. The natural aging process, however, allows a soft-fresh cheese to dry out and become stronger in flavor.

APPETIZERS and SALADS

Thin-Crust Pizza

[with Bay Scallops and Goat Cheese]

These delicious little pizzas are good served hot or at room temperature. Although most of us won't be able to cook them in a traditional wood-fired oven, a very hot conventional oven works almost as well. Topping pizza with goat cheese is a California-inspired innovation. *Makes four 10-inch pizzas; serves 6 to 8.*

---

1 cup warm water (108 degrees F)

1 package (2½ teaspoons) active dry yeast

1 teaspoon sugar

3½ cups all-purpose flour

2 teaspoons salt

6 tablespoons olive oil

½ cup cornmeal

2 cups coarsely chopped tomatoes (about 4 tomatoes)

12 ounces bay scallops (about 1½ cups)

8 ounces (1 cup) soft-fresh goat cheese

¼ cup coarsely chopped fresh basil

1 tablespoon freshly ground black pepper

In a small bowl, combine the warm water, yeast, and sugar. Let stand until foamy, about 5 minutes.

In a food processor fitted with the metal blade, combine the flour, 1 teaspoon of the salt, 3 tablespoons of the olive oil, and the yeast mixture. Process until the dough comes together into a ball, about 30 seconds. (Alternatively, combine the ingredients in a large bowl and mix with a wooden spoon.)

Transfer the dough to a floured work surface and knead until smooth and elastic, 5 to 7 minutes. Form the dough into a ball and coat lightly with about 1 teaspoon of the olive oil. Place the ball of dough in a mixing bowl, cover the bowl with a kitchen towel, and let rise in a warm place until doubled in size, about 1½ hours.

Preheat an oven to 500 degrees F.

Prepare 2 baking sheets by scattering each with ¼ cup of the cornmeal. Punch down the dough and divide into 4 equal portions. On a floured surface, roll out each portion into a round 10 inches in diameter and ⅛ inch thick. Transfer 1 round to each baking sheet; reserve the other 2 rounds for topping later. Rub a generous teaspoonful of the olive oil on the surface of the rounds, then top each round with one-fourth of the tomatoes and one-fourth of the scallops. Crumble one-fourth of the cheese over the top of each round and then sprinkle on one-fourth each of the basil and the pepper.

Bake until the cheese begins to bubble and the crusts are golden brown, 5 to 7 minutes. When done, transfer the pizzas to a cutting board or a wire rack and repeat the process with the remaining 2 dough rounds and toppings. To serve, cut each pizza into quarters and serve immediately or at room temperature.

Galette

[of Wild Mushrooms and Feta]

The piquancy of goat cheese marries well with the earthy character of wild mushrooms. A mild, not-too-salty feta is good in this dish, especially when meaty chanterelles are included in the mix. ❧ *Serves 8 to 10.*

FOR THE CRUST:

2 cups all-purpose flour

½ teaspoon salt

½ cup (1 stick) unsalted butter, chilled and cut into 8 pieces

1 egg

¼ cup milk

FOR THE FILLING:

1 tablespoon unsalted butter

2 tablespoons olive oil

4 cups (1 pound) mixed fresh wild and cultivated mushrooms such as morel, chanterelle, and portobello, cut into ½-inch-thick slices

1 teaspoon freshly ground black pepper

½ teaspoon salt (optional, as the feta may be salty enough)

½ cup dry white wine

1 tablespoon fresh thyme leaves, minced

4 ounces goats' milk feta cheese, crumbled (⅔ cup)

To make the crust, sift together the flour and salt and place in a food processor fitted with the metal blade. Add the butter and process until the mixture resembles cornmeal. Add the egg and milk and process until the dough comes together in a rough ball. (Alternatively, sift the flour and salt into a large bowl and cut in the butter with a pastry blender or 2 knives.

Add the egg and milk and stir together with a fork.) Remove the dough, wrap in waxed paper, and chill for at least 15 minutes or for up to 30 minutes.

Preheat an oven to 450 degrees F.

On a floured work surface, roll out the dough into a round 12 inches in diameter and ¼ thick. Transfer to a 10-inch tart pan, preferably with a removable bottom, pressing it gently but firmly onto the bottom and sides. Using a thumb and index finger, create an attractive edge around the rim and trim away any extra dough. Using a fork, prick a few holes in the bottom of the crust. Bake until barely golden brown, 10 to 15 minutes. Remove from the oven and place on a wire rack.

While the crust is baking, prepare the filling: In a skillet over high heat, melt the butter. As soon as it begins to foam, add the olive oil and the mushrooms and sauté until the mushrooms are well coated with the butter and oil, 2 to 3 minutes. Add the pepper, salt (if using), wine, and thyme, and continue to cook over high heat for another 1 to 2 minutes. Reduce the heat to medium and cook, stirring occasionally, until the mushrooms are tender, another 3 to 4 minutes. Remove from the heat and drain off the juices.

Spoon the mushrooms into the crust, covering the bottom evenly. Scatter the goat cheese over the mushrooms and return to the oven. Bake until the edges of the crust and the feta turn a golden brown, 10 to 15 minutes. Remove from the oven and serve at once.

Curly Endive Salad

[with Warm Goat Cheese]

In France, small heads of curly endive dressed with a mustard vinaigrette and bits of crispy bacon are traditionally served as individual salads. In this contemporary version, warm slices of goat cheese add a flavorful zip to the frizzy, pale green chicories. ❖: *Serves 4.*

FOR THE VINAIGRETTE:

2 teaspoons Dijon-style mustard

1 teaspoon red wine vinegar

¼ teaspoon salt

½ teaspoon freshly ground black pepper

⅓ cup extra-virgin olive oil

FOR THE SALADS:

6 to 8 thick slices bacon, cut crosswise into ½-inch pieces

4 small heads curly endive

1 log (4 to 6 ounces) soft-fresh goat cheese, chilled

¼ cup fine dried bread crumbs

1 tablespoon extra-virgin olive oil

½ teaspoon freshly ground black pepper

To make the **vinaigrette,** combine the mustard, vinegar, salt, and pepper in a small bowl. Mix with a fork until well blended. Very slowly drizzle in the olive oil while stirring constantly. The consistency should be very thick, like mayonnaise; you may not need the entire ⅓ cup oil. Set the vinaigrette aside.

Preheat an oven to 375 degrees F.

To make the salads, place a **skillet** over medium heat. When it is hot, add the bacon and cook, turning as needed, until crispy, 5 to 6 minutes. Remove the bacon with a slotted spoon to paper towels to drain.

To clean the **curly endives,** fill a sink with water. Remove the darker green outer wrapper leaves; discard the damaged ones and reserve any good ones for another use. Soak the chicories in the water, swirling gently as needed to remove grit and dirt that hide in the web of leaves. Remove from the water and repeat with clean water until no dirt falls from the leaves. Pass the chicories through a salad spinner or pat them dry with towels. Then turn each head upside down and, using a small paring knife, cut out the tough core. The leaves will be separated, but the heads will retain their shape; do not pull them apart. Place the heads, right side up, on individual plates.

Cut the **goat cheese** log into 4 equal disks, each 1 to 1½ inches thick. Coat the entire surface of each disk with the bread crumbs and then drizzle each disk with an equal amount of the olive oil. Place the coated disks on a baking sheet lined with aluminum foil.

Bake until heated through, 7 to 10 minutes. Remove the cheese disks from the oven and place each directly on the center of a curly endive. Drizzle the vinaigrette evenly over the top, and sprinkle each serving with an equal amount of the bacon and the pepper. Serve immediately.

Goat Cheese–Filled Cherry Tomatoes

[with Arugula]

A friend made these for her ten-year-old son, who loved them so much he requested them for dinner three times that same week. Green Grape or Yellow Pear cherry tomatoes are a good choice for this recipe. 🌱 *Serves 4.*

20 firm but ripe cherry tomatoes	*1 teaspoon red wine vinegar*
3 ounces (⅓ cup) soft-fresh goat cheese	*Salt and freshly ground black pepper*
2 teaspoons fine dried bread crumbs	*4 ounces baby arugula leaves*
2 tablespoons olive oil	

Preheat an oven to 375 degrees F.

Using a small paring knife, remove the **stems and cores** from the tomatoes. With the tip of the knife, gently scrape out the seeds to make hollowed-out shells with sturdy sides.

Spoon the **goat cheese** into the tomatoes, using about ½ teaspoon for each tomato. Transfer the stuffed tomatoes to a baking sheet or baking dish, standing them upright. Sprinkle them evenly with the bread crumbs, then drizzle the tops with 1 tablespoon of the olive oil. Bake until the tomatoes are soft but still hold their shape, 15 to 20 minutes.

Meanwhile, in a small salad bowl, **whisk** together the remaining 1 tablespoon olive oil, the vinegar, and salt and pepper to taste. Add the arugula and toss to coat evenly.

Divide the **arugula** among 4 individual plates and top each with 5 warm tomatoes. Serve at once.

Cherry Tomatoes

and

arugula

Baked Goat Cheese

[with Onion *Confit*]

The onion *confit* can be made ahead and stored in the refrigerator for up to a month. Allow it to warm to room temperature before serving. Goats' milk Camembert—wedges or small rounds—bakes well, and its rich flavor is a good complement to the confit. ❦ *Serves 6 to 8.*

FOR THE CONFIT:

2 tablespoons unsalted butter

2 pounds yellow onions, cut into
    ¼-inch-thick slices

1 tablespoon fresh thyme leaves, minced

1 teaspoon fresh winter savory or rosemary
    leaves, minced

½ teaspoon salt

1 teaspoon freshly ground black pepper

2 tablespoons olive oil

1 round (about 4 ounces) surface-ripened
    goat cheese, or a soft-fresh one if an
    aged one cannot be found

1 teaspoon olive oil

1 baguette, cut on the diagonal into
    ½-inch-thick slices

Preheat an oven to 300 degrees F.

To make the *confit,* cut the butter into chunks and place randomly on a 12-by-9-inch baking sheet or in a shallow baking dish. Heat the dish in the oven until the butter melts, about 2 minutes. Remove from the oven and place the onions in the butter, creating a layer about

1 inch deep. Sprinkle the thyme, winter savory or rosemary, salt, and pepper evenly over the onions. Finally, drizzle the olive oil over the top.

Bake for about 1½ hours, turning the onions every 15 minutes. The onions are ready when they are translucent and reduced to half their original volume. Remove the onions from the oven and set aside to cool. Reset the oven to 500 degrees F to bake the goat cheese.

Coat the entire surface of the goat cheese with the olive oil and place in a small baking dish. Bake until the surface begins to bubble and turns golden brown, 10 to 15 minutes for surface-ripened cheeses. If using a soft-fresh goat cheese, the baking time will be much shorter and the cheese will not hold its shape.

When the cheese is ready, place it on a platter with the onion *confit* and the baguette slices. Serve immediately. To eat, spread a little cheese on a bread slice and top with a forkful of onion *confit.*

Watercress and Asian Pear Salad
[w i t h   B l u e   C h e e s e]

Goats' milk blue cheese is mild and creamy, complementing the faint peppery taste of fresh watercress. If you are unable to find a goats' milk blue, use a favorite mild blue cheese or even a stronger Gorgonzola. A soft-fresh goat cheese or feta will work as well. ❧ *Serves 4.*

---

2 bunches watercress

1 Asian pear

1 teaspoon Champagne vinegar

½ teaspoon Dijon-style mustard

1 tablespoon walnut oil

2 ounces goats' milk blue cheese, crumbled (about ¼ cup)

¼ cup coarsely chopped walnuts

To prepare the watercress, remove the tough stems and discard, then rinse and dry the greens. There should be about 4 cups greens. Cut the Asian pear through the stem end into quarters and carefully cut away the core. Cut the quarters lengthwise into slices about ¹⁄₁₆ inch thick. Asian pears are quite crisp and thus somewhat fragile, so thin slices sometimes break easily. You will need to work with care. Arrange the pears in a circular pattern on a large serving plate.

In a salad bowl, combine the vinegar and mustard and mix with a fork until well blended. Slowly drizzle in the walnut oil, stirring constantly until the vinaigrette is creamy. Add the watercress to the bowl and toss until well coated.

Pile the watercress atop the pears and scatter the blue cheese over the greens. Finally, garnish the salad with the walnuts. Serve immediately.

Chiogga Beet and Shaved Crottin Salad

Reddish pink-and-white-striped Chiogga beets have a sweet, mild flavor. Unlike deep red beets, they do not turn everything they touch bright pink. The dry *crottin* adds a complementary spiciness to the slightly sweet beets. *Serves 6.*

---

5 to 6 medium-sized Chiogga beets

3 quarts water

2 tablespoons olive oil

1 tablespoon pure maple syrup

1 teaspoon balsamic vinegar

1 teaspoon minced fresh thyme

1 teaspoon minced fresh mint

1 small round (2 to 3 ounces) well-aged
crottin *cheese*

To prepare the beets, cut off the greens, leaving ½ inch of each stem intact; do not cut off the thin root ends. (Boiling the beets in their skins prevents them from bleeding and retains their flavor.) In a large saucepan, combine the beets and water and bring to a boil. Cook the beets until a sharp knife easily pierces to the center, 15 to 20 minutes. Drain and run cold water over them to halt the cooking. Let cool to room temperature. Gently slip off the skins and trim away the stems and roots. Slice the beets crosswise into ¼-inch-thick rounds.

In a large skillet over medium heat, combine the olive oil, maple syrup, and vinegar and heat until the mixture begins to foam, about 1 minute. Add the sliced beets and sauté for 3 to 4 minutes, turning frequently. Add the thyme and mint. Sauté for another minute and remove from the heat.

Arrange the beets on a serving plate in a circular pattern and, using a vegetable peeler, shave the *crottin* cheese over the top. Serve at once.

Three Dips

[f o r   A r t i c h o k e s]

Along the California coast between San Francisco and Monterey, farmers sell artichokes from roadside vegetable stands for about ten dollars a crate. We often have casual parties where we set out bowls of these tasty buds, baskets of French bread, and a selection of dips, many of them built on a base of soft-fresh goat cheese and yogurt. The dips can be prepared up to a day ahead of time. ❧ *Serves 8 to 10.*

---

5 to 6 quarts water
8 to 10 medium-sized artichokes

FOR THE THYME DIP:
½ teaspoon whole black peppercorns
1 tablespoon minced fresh thyme
1 tablespoon minced fresh Anaheim chile
2 teaspoons freshly squeezed Meyer lemon
*   juice, or 1 teaspoon other lemon juice*
4 ounces (½ cup) soft-fresh goat cheese
⅓ cup plain yogurt

FOR THE ITALIAN PARSLEY DIP:
4 ounces (½ cup) soft-fresh goat cheese
⅓ cup plain yogurt
½ cup finely minced fresh Italian parsley
¼ teaspoon salt
½ teaspoon freshly ground black pepper

FOR THE ROASTED PEPPER DIP:
1 cup minced roasted red bell peppers
8 ounces (1 cup) soft-fresh goat cheese
½ teaspoon salt
½ teaspoon freshly ground black pepper

(cont.)

In a large pot, bring the water to a rolling boil. Meanwhile, pull off any damaged outer leaves from the artichokes and trim the stem ends. Add the artichokes to the boiling water and cook until tender, 35 to 45 minutes. The artichokes are done when a leaf can easily be plucked from the base. Drain the artichokes into a colander and allow to cool.

While the artichokes are cooking, prepare the dips. For the thyme dip, in a mortar or a spice grinder, combine the peppercorns, thyme, and chile and pound or grind until a thick paste begins to form. Mix in the lemon juice. In a small bowl, combine the goat cheese, the yogurt, and the spice mixture and mix well with a fork.

For the Italian parsley dip, in a small bowl, combine the goat cheese, yogurt, parsley, salt, and pepper. Mix with a fork until well blended.

For the roasted pepper dip, in a small bowl, combine the roasted pepper, goat cheese, salt, and pepper. Mix with a fork until well blended.

To serve, arrange the artichokes in a large bowl. Place the bowls holding the dips alongside, and set out bowls in which to discard the eaten leaves.

Grilled Eggplant and Goat Cheese Rolls

This recipe calls for deep purple Japanese eggplant, but the slender, pale purple Chinese variety can be used as well. These rich and flavorful appetizers can be made several hours in advance and refrigerated. ❖ *Makes 16 to 20 rolls, serves 4 to 6.*

½ cup olive oil

½ teaspoon salt

½ teaspoon freshly ground black pepper

1 teaspoon minced fresh thyme

1 teaspoon minced fresh oregano

4 Japanese eggplants, each 4 to 5 inches long

4 ounces (½ cup) slightly aged surface-ripened goat cheese such as bûcheron

Preheat an oven to 450 degrees F.

In a medium bowl, whisk together the olive oil, salt, pepper, and herbs.

To prepare the eggplants, trim off the stems and then cut lengthwise into slices ¼ inch thick. Turn each slice in the olive oil, coating well, and place them on a baking sheet.

Bake, turning frequently, until tender and slightly browned, about 10 minutes. Remove the eggplant slices from the oven and allow to cool to room temperature.

To form the rolls, evenly spread a generous teaspoonful of the goat cheese on one side of each eggplant slice. Starting at the stem end, cheese side facing upward, roll up the slice, then pierce with a toothpick so that the roll will hold its shape.

Arrange the rolls on a platter. Serve at room temperature.

Chile and Feta Popovers

Airy popovers are an alternative to potatoes or bread, suitable for serving alongside meats or ragouts. Here the faint saltiness of the feta complements the subtle spiciness of the chiles. If the feta is overly salty, soak it in cold water for 15 to 20 minutes. ❧ *Makes 12 popovers.*

Unsalted butter and all-purpose flour
*   for popover pans*
1 cup all-purpose flour
¼ teaspoon salt
2 eggs, lightly beaten
1 cup milk

1 tablespoon melted butter
2 fresh serrano chiles, seeded and minced
3 to 4 ounces goats' milk feta cheese,
*   crumbled into pea-sized pieces*
*   (½ to ⅔ cup)*

Preheat an oven to 475 degrees F.

Grease 12 muffin cups with butter and then dust with flour, tapping out any excess.

In a medium bowl, sift together the 1 cup flour and salt. In a small bowl, gently stir together the eggs, milk, and melted butter. Fold the egg mixture into the flour mixture and stir with a fork until smooth; be careful not to overmix. The batter will be the consistency of heavy cream. Gently stir in the chiles and feta.

Pour the batter into the prepared muffin cups, dividing it evenly. They should be two-thirds full. Bake for 15 minutes, then reduce the oven temperature to 350 degrees F and continue to bake until the popovers have doubled in size and are barely browned, another 20 minutes. Remove from the oven and prick the tops. Serve immediately.

MAIN DISHES

Goat Cheese–Filled Poblanos

[with Green Tomato Salsa]

This dish draws inspiration from a trio of sources: Mexico's popular *chiles rellenos,* an abundance of summer's sweet green tomatoes, and the unique flavor of the slightly spicy poblano pepper. Experiment with different cheeses, such as a goats' milk Jack or feta. If using other than a soft-fresh cheese, coarsely grate or crumble it. 🌶 *Serves 4 to 6.*

FOR THE SALSA:

2 tomatillos, husked, peeled, and coarsely chopped

2 cloves garlic, chopped

¼ cup chopped red onion

1 fresh jalapeño chile, seeded and cut up

½ teaspoon salt

1 pound ripe green tomatoes such as Evergreen or Green Zebra, coarsely chopped

FOR THE CHILES AND BATTER:

6 fresh poblano chiles

6 ounces (¾ cup) soft-fresh goat cheese

4 eggs

½ teaspoon salt

2 tablespoons all-purpose flour

light vegetable oil for deep-frying

To make the salsa, combine the tomatillos, garlic, onion, jalapeño, and salt in a food processor fitted with the metal blade. Process until smooth. Transfer the mixture to a bowl and stir in the chopped tomatoes. Cover and chill before serving.

To prepare the chiles, cut a 2-inch slit from the middle to the stem of each pepper and gently remove the seeds; be careful not to tear the chiles. Do not remove the stems, as they hold the shape of the chile and keep the melted cheese inside. Fill each poblano with 2 tablespoons of the goat cheese and set them aside.

To make the batter, separate the eggs, putting the yolks in a small bowl and the whites in a large one. Lightly beat the yolks with a fork, then stir in the salt and the flour. Using a whisk or an electric mixer, beat the egg whites until stiff peaks form. Gently fold the yolk mixture into the whites just until no white streaks remain.

Preheat an oven to 200 degrees F. When the oven is heated, place a plate in the oven to warm.

Pour oil into a deep skillet to a depth of about 2 inches and place over a medium-high heat. The oil is ready when a tiny amount of batter dropped into it sizzles and fries instantly.

Dip the chiles, one at a time, into the batter and then, using tongs or a slotted spoon, gently lower the batter-covered chiles into the hot oil, cooking only 2 chiles at a time. When lightly browned on the first side, after about 2 minutes, turn and brown on the second side. Again using tongs or a slotted spoon, remove the lightly browned chiles from the oil, allowing them to drain over the pan briefly, and place on the warmed plate in the oven. Repeat until all the chiles are cooked.

Serve the chiles hot with the chilled salsa.

Goat Cheese and Sage Polenta
[with Fresh Tomato Sauce]

The tomato sauce can be made in the peak of summer, when tomatoes are at their best, and then frozen. What a pleasure it is to bring it out in the dead of winter and serve it atop a steaming dish of creamy goat cheese polenta. *Serves 4.*

For the tomato sauce:

3 tablespoons olive oil

2 cloves garlic, minced

2 pounds Roma tomatoes, peeled, cored,
    and coarsely chopped

2 fresh basil sprigs

½ teaspoon salt

½ teaspoon freshly ground black pepper

For the polenta:

4½ cups water

1 teaspoon salt

1 teaspoon unsalted butter

1 cup polenta

4 ounces (½ cup) soft-fresh goat cheese

1 tablespoon fresh sage leaves,
    finely chopped

To make the **tomato sauce,** in a saucepan, warm the olive oil over medium to medium-high heat. Add the garlic and sauté for 1 minute; be careful not to burn the garlic. Add the tomatoes, raise the heat to high, and cook, stirring constantly, for 5 minutes. Reduce the heat to low and add the basil, salt, and pepper. Cover and let simmer, stirring occasionally, until the sauce is thick, 45 minutes to 1 hour. Discard the basil sprigs.

About 30 minutes before the sauce is ready, begin to make the **polenta:** In a saucepan, bring the water to a rolling boil and add the salt and butter. Using a whisk, slowly stir in the polenta. It is important to stir constantly so that lumps do not form. Continue to cook over high heat, stirring constantly, until the water is fully absorbed, about 5 minutes. Reduce the heat to low and cook for another 15 minutes, continuing to stir constantly. The polenta should be thick and creamy.

Remove from the heat and stir in the goat cheese and sage. Transfer the polenta to a warmed serving bowl and let stand for 5 to 10 minutes; this allows it to solidify slightly.

To serve, spoon 3 to 4 tablespoons of the hot tomato sauce atop each serving of polenta.

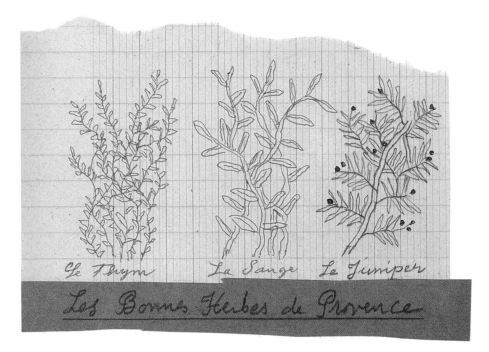

Le Thym   La Sauge   Le Juniper

Les Bonnes Herbes de Provence

Braised Rabbit

[with Creamy Red Wine and Goat Cheese Sauce]

This creamy cheese sauce, with its rich and hearty flavors, complements the flavorful meat of the rabbit. The same sauce can be served with fettuccine or roasted new potatoes. ❀ *Serves 4.*

1 rabbit, about 3 pounds, cut into 8 pieces

¼ cup all-purpose flour

2 slices bacon, cut into 1-inch pieces

4 tablespoons olive oil

1 cup minced yellow onion

1 cup minced celery (about 3 stalks)

2 bay leaves

1½ cups dry red wine

1 bunch fresh winter savory, tied together with kitchen string

3 carrots, peeled and cut into 1-inch lengths

⅓ cup chicken stock

½ cup water, if needed

1 cup shelled fava beans (about ¾ pound unshelled), immersed in boiling water for 2 to 3 minutes, drained, and peeled

8 ounces (1 cup) soft-fresh goat cheese

Preheat an oven to 275 degrees F.

Dust each piece of rabbit with the flour, coating evenly, and set aside.

In a large skillet over medium-high heat, cook the bacon until the fat is fully rendered, and add 1 tablespoon of the olive oil. Add the rabbit pieces to the pan and brown evenly on both sides, 2 to 3 minutes on each side. Remove the rabbit to a plate and set aside. Discard the bacon and olive oil.

In a deep ovenproof pot placed on the stove top, warm 2 tablespoons of the olive oil. Add the onion, celery, and bay leaves. Sauté until the celery and onions are soft and translucent, about 10 minutes. Pour in the wine and deglaze the pan by stirring to dislodge any burned bits. Bring to a boil and allow to cook until reduced by one-half, another 5 to 10 minutes. Add the winter savory, carrots, chicken stock, and rabbit, and reduce the heat to medium. Cook, uncovered, until the sauce begins to thicken, another 5 minutes. Cover and place in the preheated oven. Bake until the rabbit is tender and can be easily pierced with the tines of a fork, about 1½ hours. Check every 20 to 30 minutes to make sure there is still some liquid in the pot: if it is too dry, add the water.

When the rabbit is ready, in a small skillet over medium heat, warm the remaining 1 tablespoon olive oil. Add the fava beans and sauté until bright green and tender, 2 to 3 minutes.

Using a slotted spoon or tongs, remove the rabbit pieces to a plate and stir the fava beans and goat cheese into the sauce in the pot. Return the rabbit pieces to the sauce and serve immediately.

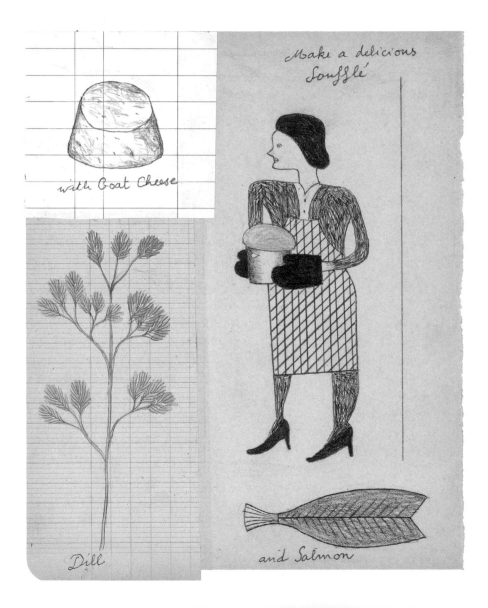

with Goat Cheese

Dill

Make a delicious Soufflé

and Salmon

Soufflé of Goat Cheese,

[Smoked Salmon, and Dill]

The classic combination of salmon and dill is rendered even more irresistible when baked with just a hint of goat cheese flavor. Serve piping hot, or let cool and enjoy as a special late-night snack. ❧• *Serves 6 to 8.*

¼ cup (½ stick) unsalted butter

¼ cup all-purpose flour

1 cup milk

½ teaspoon salt

½ teaspoon freshly ground black pepper

8 ounces (1 cup) soft-fresh goat cheese

½ cup finely chopped smoked salmon

⅓ cup finely chopped fresh dill

4 eggs

Preheat an oven to 300 degrees F.

Butter a standard (1½-quart) souffle dish.

In a saucepan over a medium heat, melt the butter. When it begins to foam, whisk in the flour until a paste forms, about 30 seconds. Immediately whisk in ¼ cup of the milk and reduce the heat to low. Whisking continuously, add the remaining ¾ cup milk and the salt and pepper. When the sauce has thickened, after about 5 minutes, stir in the goat cheese. Continue to stir until the cheese is completely blended into the sauce, about 1 minute.

(cont.)

Remove the sauce from the heat and stir in the salmon and dill. Allow to cool slightly.

Meanwhile, separate the eggs, putting the yolks in a small bowl and the whites in a large one. Lightly beat the yolks until well blended. Using a whisk or an electric mixer, beat the whites until stiff peaks form.

When the sauce has cooled somewhat, stir in the egg yolks. Then gently fold the cheese sauce into the egg whites just until no white streaks remain. Do not overmix or you will deflate the soufflé. Pour the mixture into the prepared soufflé dish.

Bake until the soufflé is golden brown and nearly doubled in size, 35 to 40 minutes. Remove from the oven and serve immediately.

Pasta Salad

[with Basil, Sungold Cherry Tomatoes, and Goat Cheese]

Perfect for a lazy summer lunch, this simple mix of the season's harvest needs only a salad of mixed greens or an array of grilled garden vegetables to round out the meal. *Serves 6 to 8.*

2 teaspoons salt

4 tablespoons extra-virgin olive oil

1 pound dried rotelli *or similar pasta*

2 cups (about 12 ounces) Sungold or other
cherry tomatoes, cut in half

1 cup coarsely chopped fresh basil

8 ounces (1 cup) soft-fresh goat cheese

1 teaspoon freshly ground black pepper

Bring a large pot of **water** to a rolling boil. Add 1 teaspoon of the salt and 1 tablespoon of the olive oil and then the pasta. Cook, stirring occasionally, until al dente, 7 to 10 minutes or according to the package instructions. Be careful not to overcook. Drain into a colander.

Transfer the **pasta** to a large serving bowl and add the remaining 3 tablespoons olive oil, the tomatoes, and basil. Crumble the goat cheese over the top and toss all the ingredients together, adding the remaining 1 teaspoon salt and the pepper.

Serve the salad warm or at room temperature.

Peppered Rib-eye Steak

[with Chanterelles and Goat Cheese Sauce]

In Provence, restaurants often serve this specialty with a creamy wild mushroom sauce, such as chanterelles in the fall and morels in the spring. The goat cheese sauce, however, is our own addition. ❧ *Serves 2.*

2 rib-eye steaks, each 4 ounces and
   ¾ inch thick
1 tablespoon coarsely ground black pepper
2 tablespoons unsalted butter
1 tablespoon olive oil
4 ounces fresh chanterelle mushrooms,
   coarsely chopped

1 tablespoon minced fresh oregano
1 tablespoon all-purpose flour
1 cup milk
½ teaspoon salt
4 ounces (½ cup) soft-fresh goat cheese

Generously coat each steak on both sides with the cracked pepper and let stand at room temperature for about 15 minutes.

In a skillet over medium heat, melt 1 tablespoon of the butter with the olive oil. When the mixture begins to foam, add the mushrooms and oregano and sauté until the mushrooms are tender and the juices have begun to flow, 3 to 4 minutes. Remove from the heat and set aside.

Preheat a broiler.

In a small saucepan over medium heat, melt the remaining 1 tablespoon of butter. When it begins to foam, whisk in the flour until a paste forms, about 30 seconds. Immediately whisk in ¼ cup of the milk and reduce the heat to low. Whisking continuously, gradually add the remaining ¾ cup milk and the salt. When the sauce has thickened, after about 5 minutes, stir in the goat cheese until it melts and the sauce is smooth, about 1 minute. Remove from the heat and stir in the mushrooms. Set the sauce aside and cover to keep warm.

Place the steaks in a shallow flameproof baking dish or on a broiler pan. Slip the dish or pan into the broiler about 3 inches from the heat and broil, turning once, for 3 minutes on each side for medium-rare. You may wish to cook the steaks a little less or a little more, depending upon personal taste.

While the steaks are cooking, reheat the sauce over low heat if it has cooled. When the steaks are ready, immediately transfer to warmed individual plates and spoon the sauce generously atop each one. Serve at once.

Potato and White Cheddar Gratin

Perfect for those who love a good, old-fashioned potato dish, this gratin can be served as a main course with salad or as an accompaniment to a juicy grilled steak. ❧ *Serves 6.*

---

3 quarts water

2 pounds Yukon Gold or other yellow-fleshed potatoes, peeled and cut into ¼-inch-thick rounds

1 tablespoon unsalted butter

1 tablespoon all-purpose flour

1 cup milk

1 teaspoon salt

10 ounces goats' milk white Cheddar cheese, shredded (about 2 cups)

1 tablespoon olive oil

2 cloves garlic, crushed

1 teaspoon freshly ground black pepper

Preheat an oven to 400 degrees F.

The potatoes need to be **parboiled** before they are baked, but it is important not to overcook them during this step. In a large pot, bring the water to a boil. Add the potatoes and cook until barely tender when pricked with the tines of a fork, 3 to 4 minutes. Drain into a colander and then run cold water over the potatoes for a couple of minutes to halt the cooking.

In a small saucepan over medium heat, melt the butter. When it begins to foam, whisk in the flour until a paste forms, about 30 seconds. Immediately whisk in ¼ cup of the milk and reduce the heat to low. Whisking continuously, gradually add the remaining ¾ cup milk. When the sauce has thickened, after about 5 minutes, stir in 1 cup of the cheese until it melts and the sauce is smooth, about 1 minute. Remove from the heat and set aside.

Select a 1½-quart baking dish, preferably round or oval, with 2½- to 3-inch sides. Rub the dish first with the olive oil and then with the garlic. Discard the garlic. Cover the bottom of the dish with potato slices, arranging them in a single layer and slightly overlapping them. Drizzle about 2 tablespoons of the sauce evenly over the layer. Repeat the layering and the drizzling with the sauce until you have used all the potatoes and the dish is full. Pour the remaining sauce around the edges of the potatoes and across the top. Scatter the remaining 1 cup cheese over the surface and then sprinkle with the pepper.

La Chèvrerie

Bake until the top begins to bubble and brown, 35 to 40 minutes. Serve hot or at room temperature.

Gnocchi

[with Spinach and Goat Cheese]

This is inspired by an old family friend who always made gnocchi on Sundays. But unlike her version, this dish is light and free of rich sauces, although certainly not lacking in flavor. *Serves 6.*

2½ pounds russet potatoes, peeled

1 egg

1½ cups all-purpose flour, plus flour for
    working the dough

2 teaspoons salt

4 quarts water

3 tablespoons olive oil

½ yellow onion, minced

2 cloves garlic, minced

1 bunch spinach, stemmed and finely
    chopped

6 ounces (¾ cup) soft-fresh goat cheese

In a **large pot,** combine the potatoes and cold water to cover them generously. Bring to a rolling boil over high heat and boil until the potatoes are tender and can easily be pierced with the tines of a fork, about 15 minutes. Drain well and then run cold water over the potatoes to halt the cooking. When cool enough to handle, using the large holes of a grater, grate the potatoes into a bowl.

Add the egg, flour, and ½ teaspoon of the salt to the potatoes and mix well until a sticky dough forms, 3 to 5 minutes. Turn out onto a well-floured work surface and knead until the dough is soft and somewhat sticky, about 5 minutes. It is important to keep the work surface and the dough well floured or the gnocchi will stick together when cooked. Working with about 1 cup of the dough at a time, use floured palms to roll it back and forth on the work surface to form a log 12 inches long. Cut the log in half crosswise, and, using the same technique, roll each half into a log 12 inches long. Cut each log into ½-inch-long pieces. Coat each piece thoroughly with flour. Repeat with the remaining dough, setting the pieces aside on a baking sheet as they are formed.

Bring a large pot of water to a **rolling boil.** Add 1 teaspoon of the salt and about 2 dozen gnocchi to the boiling water. Cook until they float to the top, about 2 minutes. Remove with a slotted spoon and transfer to a bowl. Cook the remaining gnocchi in the same manner. When all of the gnocchi have been cooked, toss them with 1 tablespoon of the olive oil.

Preheat an oven to 500 degrees F.

In a **large skillet** over a medium heat, warm 1 tablespoon of the olive oil. Add the onion and garlic and sauté until translucent, 3 to 4 minutes. Add the spinach and toss gently with the onions and garlic until slightly wilted, about 30 seconds. Remove from the heat and transfer to a large bowl.

Add the **gnocchi** and the cheese to the spinach mixture. Mix together gently but thoroughly, and transfer to a shallow baking dish just large enough to hold the mixture. Drizzle the top with the remaining 1 tablespoon olive oil and sprinkle with the remaining ½ teaspoon salt. Bake until the cheese begins to brown, about 15 minutes. Serve immediately.

Sautéed Chard Threads

[with Feta]

Quick to prepare, this vegetarian dish can be served atop pasta or polenta. During the winter, leafy greens are available in abundance; experiment with substituting red or green mustard, kale, red chard or even spinach for the green chard. ❧ *Serves 4.*

---

1 large bunch green Swiss chard with stalks intact

3 tablespoons olive oil

2 cloves garlic, minced

¼ cup chicken or vegetable stock

½ teaspoon salt

½ teaspoon freshly ground black pepper

3 to 4 ounces goats' milk feta cheese, coarsely crumbled (½ to ⅔ cup)

To prepare the **chard,** cut out the white stalk, or spine, in each leaf by cutting along either side of it, creating a V shape. Coarsely chop the stalks and set them aside. Stack the leaves, one on top of the other, and roll them up, creating a log. Cut the log crosswise into ½-inch-wide sections. When the sections are unfurled, they will form long, narrow strips.

Heat the **olive oil** in a large skillet over high heat. Add the garlic and chopped chard stalks and sauté until tender, about 5 minutes. Add the stock and allow to cook down for 1 to 2 minutes. Reduce the heat to medium and mix in the chard leaves, salt, and pepper. When the leaves just begin to wilt, after 1 to 2 minutes, fold in the feta cheese. When the cheese begins to soften, after about 1 minute, remove from the heat. Transfer to a serving dish and serve immediately.

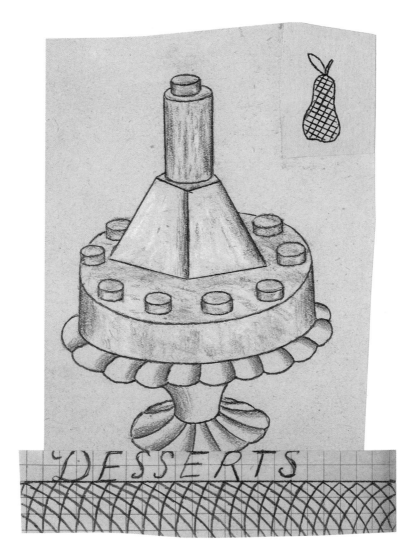

DESSERTS

Lemon Cheesecake

When we lived in Provence, a neighbor and fellow cheese maker made lemon cheesecake from *fromage blanc*. It was baked in a wood-fired oven, as few of us at that time had gas or electricity, and the resulting texture was wonderfully light and crumbly. 🍃 *Serves 10 to 12.*

FOR THE CRUST:	FOR THE FILLING:
1½ cups pecan halves	*1¼ pounds (2½ cups) soft-fresh goat cheese*
¼ cup loosely packed light brown sugar	*12 ounces (1½ cups)* mascarpone *cheese*
20 plain water crackers, broken into	*3 tablespoons finely grated lemon zest*
1-inch pieces	*4 eggs, lightly beaten*
½ teaspoon freshly grated nutmeg	*1⅓ cups granulated sugar*
6 tablespoons unsalted butter, melted	*½ teaspoon salt*

To make the **crust,** in a food processor fitted with the metal blade, combine the pecans, brown sugar, crackers, and nutmeg. Process until finely ground. Add the melted butter, and continue to process until the mixture is moist and sticks to the sides of the processor bowl. Gather the mixture together and place in the center of a 9- or 10-inch springform pan. Using your fingertips, gently press the crumb mixture evenly over the bottom and halfway up the sides of the pan. Set aside.

Preheat an oven to 350 degrees F.

To make the **filling,** rinse out the food processor bowl, then again fit it with the metal blade. Add the goat cheese, *mascarpone* cheese, lemon zest, eggs, granulated sugar, and salt. Process until smooth and creamy. Pour the mixture into the prepared springform pan. Place on a baking sheet, as the filling sometimes leaks through the seams of the pan.

Bake until the top springs back when lightly pressed with a fingertip, about 1 hour. Remove from the oven and place on a wire rack in the refrigerator to cool for at least 1 hour. When completely cool, release the sides of the springform pan and transfer the cheesecake to a serving plate. Serve chilled or at room temperature.

A Beautiful Presentation

Homemade Plum Preserves

[over Goat Cheese]

This is a traditional French dessert or breakfast dish. Usually it is just a serving of pure goats' milk *fromage blanc,* but since the cheese is difficult to find outside of France, here we have combined any easily purchased soft-fresh goat cheese with crème fraîche to mimic the flavor. ❦ *Serves 6 to 8.*

---

*3 cups (about 2 pounds) ripe plums,
    any variety, peeled, pitted, and cut
    into ½-inch-thick slices*
¾ cup sugar

½ cup water
1 tablespoon finely grated lemon zest
8 ounces (1 cup) soft-fresh goat cheese
1 cup crème fraîche

In a saucepan, stir together the plums, sugar, water, and lemon zest. Bring to a rolling boil over high heat, stirring occasionally. When the mixture begins to foam and is about to bubble over, reduce the heat to medium and spoon off the foam. Cook, uncovered, for 15 minutes. Then cover, reduce the heat to low, and cook until a thick layer of foam develops on the top, 25 to 30 minutes. Remove from the heat, skim away and discard the foam, and transfer to a bowl. Let cool to room temperature.

In a small bowl, whisk together the goat cheese and crème fraîche until smooth.

For each serving, spoon an equal amount of the cheese mixture onto a small dessert plate. Top with equal amounts of the plum preserves. Serve at once.

Cheese and Seasonal Fruit Platter

Fruit and cheese generally constitute family dessert in France, except on special occasions. We suggest a simple selection of different types of goat cheeses, such as a blue or a mold-ripened Banon and an aged *crottin*. In the summer, fill the platter with peaches, nectarines, and berries; in fall, provide pears, apples, and figs. Alter the fruits and cheeses suggested here as you like. 🎋 *Serves 4 to 6.*

FOR THE CHEESES:

1 round (about 4 ounces) soft-fresh goat
  cheese
1 wedge (2 to 3 ounces) goats' milk blue
  cheese
1 Banon cheese wrapped in brown
  chestnut leaves (about 4 ounces)

FOR THE FRUITS:

2 Bartlett pears
2 French or Italian butter pears
1 tablespoon freshly squeezed lemon juice
8 to 10 very ripe Black Mission figs

Make sure all the cheeses are served at **room temperature.** Slice all the pears lengthwise into eighths, carefully cut away the cores, and rub with the lemon juice to prevent browning. The figs can be served whole or cut in half.

Arrange the fruits on a dessert platter with the cheeses. Serve at the end of any meal.

Poached Winter Pears

[with Sweet Goat Cheese]

Here, a scoop of sweet cheese sits in the center of a soft poached pear, with a scattering of finely chopped fresh mint over the top. ❧ *Serves 4.*

2 tablespoons unsalted butter

*4 medium-sized Bartlett pears, halved
    lengthwise, peeled, and cored*

¼ cup brandy

1 cup water, or as needed

8 ounces (1 cup) soft-fresh goat cheese

1 tablespoon finely chopped fresh mint

In a skillet over high heat, melt the butter. Be careful not to let it burn. When it begins to foam, reduce the heat to medium and add the pears. Sauté until they begin soften, 3 to 4 minutes. Pour in the brandy and turn the pears in the liquid for another 2 to 3 minutes. Add 1 cup water, cover, and simmer over medium heat until the pears are tender and can be easily pierced with the tines of a fork, about 10 minutes. Check the water after a few minutes and add more if necessary; it should be about ½ inch deep.

Remove from the heat and place 2 pear halves, hollow sides up, on each dessert plate. Spoon about 2 tablespoons of the goat cheese in the hollow of each half and sprinkle with the mint. Serve immediately.

Baked Apples

[with Golden Raisins and Goat Cheese]

The marriage of savory and sweet ingredients in a dessert creates an intriguing combination. Use your favorite baking apples, tart or mellow, for this dish. ❖ *Serves 6.*

6 apples

10 ounces (1¼ cups) soft-fresh goat cheese

½ cup firmly packed brown sugar

½ cup golden raisins

¼ cup slivered blanched almonds, toasted

Preheat an oven to 375 degrees F.

Using a small paring knife, remove the core from each apple to within about ½ inch of the bottom. Be careful not to cut all the way through to the bottom. Using a small spoon, scoop out a cavity in the center of the apple about 1½ inches in diameter and 2 inches deep. Set aside.

In a small bowl, combine the goat cheese and brown sugar and stir until smooth. Add the raisins and stir to combine. Spoon the mixture into the hollowed-out apples, dividing it evenly and mounding it so that it barely rises above the tops. Sprinkle the almonds evenly over the filling. Select a baking dish large enough to hold the apples snugly and line it with aluminum foil. Place the apples in the dish.

Bake, uncovered, until the filling and almonds brown and the apples are very soft, as if about to collapse, about 45 minutes. Serve hot.

LIST OF RESOURCES

CAPRIOL, INC.
P.O. Box 117
Greenville, IN 47124
Tel: (812) 923-9408

CHICORY FARM
P.O. Box 25
Mount Herman, LA 70450
Tel: (800) 605-4550

FROMAGERIE BELL CHÈVRE INC.
26910 Bethel Road
Elkmont, AL 35620
Tel: (205) 423-2238

GOAT'S LEAP CHEESE
Saint Helena, CA
Tel: (707) 963-2337
Fax: (707) 963-2337

JUNIPER GROVE FARM
Redmond, OR 97756
Tel: (888) FROMAGE

LITTLE RAINBOW CHÈVRE
15 Doe Hill
Hillsdale, NY 12529
Tel: (518) 325-GOAT

REDWOOD HILL FARM
Sebastopol, CA
Tel: (707) 823-8250
Fax: (707) 823-6976

VERMONT BUTTER AND CHEESE
COMPANY
P.O. Box 95
Websterville, VT 05678
Tel: (802) 479-9371, (800) VTGOATS

WESTFIELD FARM
28 Worcester Road
Hubbardston, MA 01452
Tel: (508) 928-5110
Fax: (508) 928-5745

WILLAMETTE VALLEY CHÈVRE
(produced by Tall Talk Dairy)
11961 South Emerson Road
Canby, OR 97013
Tel: (800) 343-GOAT

Index

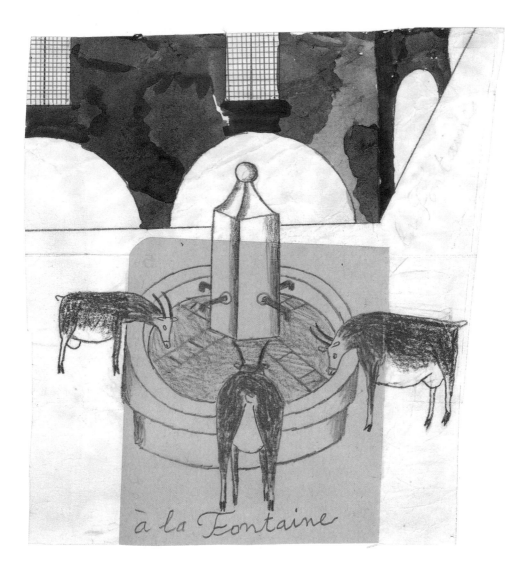

à la Fontaine

Table of Equivalents

[The exact equivalents in the following tables have been rounded for convenience.]

US/UK	WEIGHTS		TEMPERATURES		
oz = ounce	*US/UK*	*Metric*	*Fahrenheit*	*Celsius*	*Gas*
lb = pound	1 oz	30 g	250	120	½
in = inch	2 oz	60 g	275	140	1
ft = foot	3 oz	90 g	300	150	2
tbl = tablespoon	4 oz (¼ lb)	125 g	325	160	3
fl oz = fluid ounce	5 oz (⅓ lb)	155 g	350	180	4
qt = quart	6 oz	185 g	375	190	5
	7 oz	220 g	400	200	6
METRIC	8 oz (½ lb)	250 g	425	220	7
g = gram	10 oz	315 g	450	230	8
kg = kilogram	12 oz (¾ lb)	375 g	475	240	9
mm = millimeter	14 oz	440 g	500	260	10
cm = centimeter	16 oz (1 lb)	500 g			
ml = milliliter	1½ lb	750 g			
l = liter	2 lb	1 kg			
	3 lb	1.5 kg